ISLAMISM
AND THE FUTURE OF
THE CHRISTIANS OF THE
MIDDLE EAST

HERBERT AND JANE DWIGHT WORKING GROUP
ON ISLAMISM AND THE INTERNATIONAL ORDER

*Many of the writings associated with this
Working Group will be published by the
Hoover Institution. Materials published to date,
or in production, are listed below.*

ESSAYS

Saudi Arabia and the New Strategic Landscape
Joshua Teitelbaum

Islamism and the Future of the Christians of the Middle East
Habib C. Malik

Syria through Jihadist Eyes: A Perfect Enemy
Nibras Kazimi

The Ideological Struggle for Pakistan
Ziad Haider

BOOKS

Freedom or Terror: Europe Faces Jihad
Russell A. Berman

ISLAMISM AND THE FUTURE OF THE CHRISTIANS OF THE MIDDLE EAST

Habib C. Malik

HOOVER INSTITUTION PRESS
Stanford University   Stanford, California

www.hoover.org

Hoover Institution Press Publication No. 585

Hoover Institution at Leland Stanford Junior University, Stanford, California, 94305-6010

First printing 2010
16   15   14   13   12   11   10   9   8   7   6   5   4   32   1

Manufactured in the United States of America

The paper used in this publication meets the minimum Requirements of the American National Standard for Information Sciences—Permanence of Paper for Printed Library Materials, ANSI/NISO Z39.48-1992. ∞

Cataloging-in-Publication Data is available from the Library of Congress.
ISBN 978-0-8179-1095-2 (pbk.)
ISBN 978-0-8179-1096-9 (e-book)

The Hoover Institution gratefully acknowledges
the following individuals and foundations
for their significant support of the

HERBERT AND JANE DWIGHT WORKING GROUP
ON ISLAMISM AND THE INTERNATIONAL ORDER

Herbert and Jane Dwight
Stephen Bechtel Foundation
Lynde and Harry Bradley Foundation
Mr. and Mrs. Clayton W. Frye Jr.
Lakeside Foundation

CONTENTS

Foreword

FOR DECADES, the themes of the Hoover Institution have revolved around the broad concerns of political and economic and individual freedom. The cold war that engaged and challenged our nation during the twentieth century guided a good deal of Hoover's work, including its archival accumulation and research studies. The steady output of work on the communist world offers durable testimonies to that time, and struggle. But there is no repose from history's exertions, and no sooner had communism left the stage of history than a huge challenge arose in the broad lands of the Islamic world. A brief respite, and a meandering road, led from the fall of the Berlin Wall on 11/9 in 1989 to 9/11. Hoover's newly launched project, the Herbert and Jane Dwight Working Group on

Islamism and the International Order, is our contribution to a deeper understanding of the struggle in the Islamic world between order and its nemesis, between Muslims keen to protect the rule of reason and the gains of modernity, and those determined to deny the Islamic world its place in the modern international order of states. The United States is deeply engaged, and dangerously exposed, in the Islamic world, and we see our working group as part and parcel of the ongoing confrontation with the radical Islamists who have declared war on the states in their midst, on American power and interests, and on the very order of the international state system.

The Islamists are doubtless a minority in the world of Islam. But they are a determined breed. Their world is the Islamic emirate, led by self-styled "emirs and mujahedeen in the path of God" and legitimized by the pursuit of the caliphate that collapsed with the end of the Ottoman Empire in 1924. These masters of terror and their foot soldiers have made it increasingly difficult to integrate the world of Islam into modernity. In the best of worlds, the entry of Muslims into modern culture and economics would have presented difficulties of no small consequence: the strictures on women, the legacy of humiliation and self-pity, the outdated educational systems, and an explosive demography that is forever at war with social and economic gains. But the borders these warriors of the faith have erected between Islam and "the other" are particularly forbidding. The lands of Islam were the lands of a crossroads civilization, trading routes and mixed populations. The Islamists have waged war, and a brutally effective one it has to be conceded, against that civilizational inheritance. The leap into the modern world economy as attained by China and India in recent years will be virtually impossible in a culture that feeds off belligerent self-pity, and endlessly calls for wars of faith.

The war of ideas with radical Islamism is inescapably central to this Hoover endeavor. The strategic context of this clash, the landscape of that Greater Middle East, is the other pillar. We face three layers of danger in the heartland of the Islamic world: states that have succumbed to the sway of terrorists in which state authority no longer exists (Afghanistan, Somalia, and Yemen), dictatorial regimes that suppress their people at home and pursue deadly weapons of mass destruction and adventurism abroad (Iraq under Saddam Hussein, the Iranian theocracy), and "enabler" regimes, such as the ones in Egypt and Saudi Arabia, which export their own problems with radical Islamism to other parts of the Islamic world and beyond. In this context, the task of reversing Islamist radicalism and of reforming and strengthening the state across the entire Muslim world—the Middle East, Africa, as well as South, Southeast, and Central Asia—is the greatest strategic challenge of the twenty-first century. The essential starting point is detailed knowledge of our enemy.

Thus, the working group will draw on the intellectual resources of Hoover and Stanford and on an array of scholars and practitioners from elsewhere in the United States, from the Middle East, and the broader world of Islam. The scholarship on contemporary Islam can now be read with discernment. A good deal of it, produced in the immediate aftermath of 9/11, was not particularly deep and did not stand the test of time and events. We, however, are in the favorable position of a "second generation" assessment of that Islamic material. Our scholars and experts can report, in a detailed, authoritative way, on Islam within the Arabian Peninsula, on trends within Egyptian Islam, on the struggle between the Kemalist secular tradition in Turkey, and on the new Islamists, particularly the fight for the loyalty of European Islam between these who accept the canon, and the discipline, of modernism and those who don't.

Arabs and Muslims need not be believers in American exceptionalism, but our hope is to engage them in this contest of ideas. We will not necessarily aim at producing primary scholarship, but such scholarship may materialize in that our participants are researchers who know their subjects intimately. We see our critical output as essays accessible to a broader audience, primers about matters that require explication, op-eds, writings that will become part of the public debate, and short, engaging books that can illuminate the choices and the struggles in modern Islam.

We see this endeavor as a faithful reflection of the values that animate a decent, moderate society. We know the travails of modern Islam, and this working group will be unsparing in depicting them. But we also know that the battle for modern Islam is not yet lost, that there are brave men and women fighting to retrieve their faith from the extremists. Some of our participants will themselves be intellectuals and public figures who have stood up to the pressure. The working group will be unapologetic about America's role in the Muslim world. A power that laid to waste religious tyranny in Afghanistan and despotism in Iraq, that came to the rescue of the Muslims in the Balkans when they appeared all but doomed, has given much to those burdened populations. We haven't always understood Islam and Muslims—hence this inquiry. But it is a given of the working group that the pursuit of modernity and human welfare, and of the rule of law and reason, in Islamic lands is the common ground between America and contemporary Islam.

THIS ESSAY by the noted Lebanese scholar Habib Malik is a unique and melancholic account of the fate of the Christians of the Middle East in the era of Islamist radicalism. Himself a child of Christian Lebanon with an American education, Professor Malik writes of the cruel irony of Christianity besieged in the land of its birth. Christianity may have "won the world," he observes, but it is on the run in its birthplace. The tyranny of demography is at work: Christians are leaving their homelands in Egypt, the Levant, and Iraq in record numbers, and their birthrates are also lower than those in the Muslim communities. Islamist extremism has frightened and delegitimized those Christians, written them off as "fifth columnists" of the West. But ironically (and this lies at the heart of Professor Malik's lament) the powers in the West have scant interest in the fate of Christians in the East. The spectacle that this learned essay presents is not pretty. But it is important to document unsparingly the ordeal of the Christian Arabs in this time of Islamist radicalism. In an ideal world, those Christians would have been a bridge between the lands of

Islam and the civilization of the West. But the ground is ablaze, and bridges don't fare well in a time of civilizational wars.

Fouad Ajami
Senior Fellow, Hoover Institution
Co-chairman, Herbert and Jane Dwight Working Group on Islamism and the International Order

ISLAMISM AND THE FUTURE OF THE CHRISTIANS OF THE MIDDLE EAST

HABIB C. MALIK

I. STRAINED TO THE BREAKING POINT

THAT THE MIDDLE EAST is the cradle of the world's three monotheisms is a phrase one encounters in every high-school textbook or tourist brochure about the region. But this fact alone reveals little about present-day conditions that see two of the three great religions thriving in their geographic points of origin while the third, Christianity, appears in a state of terminal regional decline. Islam, since the days of its early and spectacular conquests from Morocco to Indonesia and beyond, has had both the overwhelming numbers and the territory to show for itself. As an essentially martial religion, Islam has achieved phenomenal success in capturing and holding its place of birth as well as wrenching lands far and wide from the sway of rival belief systems. It faces daunting challenges from modernity but no existential fears of eradication from where it started or from the wider regional circumference. Judaism, despite eschewing converts and undergoing a momentous historic scattering into a prolonged Diaspora, managed to survive in pockets and niches throughout the Middle East, withstanding often severe pressures from its two other offspring religions. Until, that is, a secular Jewish nationalism—Zionism—was born in nineteenth-century Europe and magnetically reassembled its people along with their ancient creed, language, customs, and everything else they had acquired, or honed, over two millennia into the formidable achievement that is Israel today. They may still not have the numbers, but they certainly do possess both the strength and external support to sustain themselves seemingly indefinitely in their precise place of origin: the land of milk and honey glimpsed by Moses over three millennia ago from Mount Nebo.

For its part Christianity may have surely "won the world" in the sense of being the most widespread religion in history with the largest number of adherents, but it is steadily losing ground in and around its birthplace. Why is that? Today, between 10–12 million native Christians remain in the Middle East, concentrated mainly in Egypt, the Levant (Jordan, Lebanon, Syria and the Palestine territories), and Iraq. Their numbers, however, continue to dwindle due to a variety of factors, both internal and external. Most prominent among the outside sources of pressure has been the rise in recent decades of Islamic extremism, or Islamism, in both its Sunni and Shiite varieties. This is only the latest among potentially calamitous dangers besetting Middle Eastern Christians, not least because it tends to stir ancient antagonisms and revive atavistic rejections of the different other as the despised infidel.

Taking the longer historical view, it becomes apparent that Christianity had begun to exhaust its meager reservoir of hospitality in the Near East and Arabia toward the end of the first millennium, during the adolescent period of the new faith. This faith, which claimed that God Himself became a man so that all humans may be saved from their sins, was never able to find sustained easy acceptance nor permanent fertile soil in the Middle East where it first appeared—a mystery that is perhaps partially explained as confirmation of the familiar adage that no prophet receives honor in his place of origin among his people. For, according to the new message, the "Good News" amounted to this: In the end what counts are not divine words or laws or rituals, but that everyone is invited to have an intimate individual as well as communal relationship with the living person of the Incarnate God—Jesus of Nazareth, the Christ, the Word, the Son of God, the Savior through whom all things were made. This is humanity's only hope and all else is trivial.

First came rejection by the Sanhedrin in ancient Jerusalem; then three centuries of brutal suppression by pagan Romans; then, after the church had triumphed over the empire, a string of heresiarchs emerged, some of whose followers retreated into the desert fringes only to return with a vengeance in the seventh century as Islamic conquerors. The Christian creed they rejected had proven too much to bear for these desert folk who were usually beyond the reach of the imperial centers of power with which the destiny of the church in the East had become fatefully intertwined. There followed a prolonged severing of the region from the dynamism of the Western church with the only, and catastrophic, contacts coming in the form of the Crusades—a delayed Western reaction to the earlier Islamic conquests that had reached southern France.

Not only were some Christians branded as fifth columnists during the Crusader period, but persecutions mounted after the Mongol invasions, especially when the Mongols embraced Islam. The fall of Constantinople in 1453 to the besieging armies of Ottoman Sultan Mohammad the Conqueror was a watershed in the history of eastern Christianity because the

Christians of Asia Minor never recovered from that loss, and the rest of Levantine Christianity was severely weakened as a result. Massacres resumed against these Christian communities, including Armenians and Assyrians beginning in the second half of the nineteenth century and on into the 1930s. A brief respite occurred with the emergence of Arab nationalism as a unifying secular ideology during the middle decades of the twentieth century only to see the old perils return with the onset of this latest Islamist wave.

Given this toxic historical residue it is no surprise that precariously subsisting Middle Eastern Christian communities today face adverse consequences of existential proportions when militant ideologies like Jihadism begin to run amok. The Christian faith that had started out long ago as "a stumbling block for the Jews and absurdity for the Greeks" also became blasphemy for the Muslims, and it has not been too difficult for Islamist radicals to resuscitate this primordial repulsion from Christianity latent within Political Islam and adorn it with a violent disposition.[1] If forced or gradual conversions were the leading factors that diminished Christian numbers throughout the Middle East during the centuries following the early Islamic conquests, emigration has become the principal avenue in the last one hundred years or so through which the native Christian population is being culled, and this hemorrhaging by an exodus of individuals, families, and whole communities proceeds unabated. Suspicion of the West—prevalent in much of the Islamic world and often transformed into outright hatred because of the ravages attributed to Western colonialism and imperialism and unqualified support for Israel—has also served on occasion as a pretext to scapegoat indigenous Christians because they have been perceived as sharing the same religious beliefs with the vilified Westerners.

As this attrition of the region's Christians accelerates, the lingering impression in the outside world is that what remains of these communities amounts to nothing more than vanishing relics of the past. The relic phenomenon is an alarming one and the numbers offer sobering evidence of its impending reality. In 1948 Jerusalem was about a fifth Christian;

today, it is less than 2 percent. For centuries Christians used to constitute over 80 percent of Bethlehem's population, but today they are barely a third and falling. In 1943, at the time of its independence, Lebanon was a majority-Christian country, but after thirty years of war and foreign occupation Lebanon's Christians now make up around a third of the population and the trend is demographic contraction. It is estimated that about half of Iraq's 1.4 million Christians have fled the country since the American invasion in 2003.[2]

Accepting the relic status of Middle Eastern Christianity betrays at best a cold indifference and at worst complicity in the ongoing extinction. There are objective reasons why a Muslim-majority Middle East that nevertheless continues to exhibit pluralist acceptance of its non-Muslim indigenous communities regardless of their demographic size or geographic spread is a healthier Middle East that is less prone to extremism. As Pope Benedict XVI put it when he visited Jerusalem in May 2009, "great cultural and spiritual impoverishment" results when the Christian inhabitants of the city, and of the region as a whole, depart in significant numbers.[3] Reversing this trend will be an awesome undertaking.

The prescription to "love your enemies" may have been too difficult for the East to stomach and with time many Christians sadly became converted to the hate and vengeance ensconced in other creeds—thus has been the way of the world most everywhere.[4] But, on balance, Christians native to the Middle East have generally exhibited a greater docility and lack of belligerence than their coreligionists in the Christian world at large, except under specific circumstances when they did opt to defend themselves against external attack. Their story, the trials they face, their options, and their prospects are explored in the pages ahead.

II. TWO NARRATIVES

President Obama's celebrated speech addressing the Muslim world and delivered in Cairo on June 4, 2009, was well received and has helped to improve America's image in the eyes of many Muslims globally.[5] In the course of the speech there is a passing reference that is directly germane to the present discussion. The President extols "the richness of religious diversity," adding "whether it is for Maronites in Lebanon or the Copts in Egypt." Obviously, the president's speechwriter had good intentions in lumping together in one breath those two quite different Middle Eastern Christian communities, although mentioning the Maronites so prominently three days before Lebanon's then watershed parliamentary elections was designed to signal strong U.S. support for the pro-American stance taken by the Maronite Patriarch, the spiritual leader of Lebanon's largest Christian denomination. And mention of the Copts clearly aimed to remind the world that the President had not forgotten a religious community that in recent years had experienced repeated bouts of attacks from fanatics while the Egyptian authorities either watched from the sidelines or tacitly condoned the abuse. What seems to have been overlooked—and it is a fine yet pivotal nuance—is the slightly negative impact such a joining in a single reference of the two communities, Maronites and Copts, would have mainly on Maronites and other Christians in Lebanon. Not to mention how the conspicuous absence of any reference to Iraq's Christians, suffering grievously since America's 2003 invasion of their country, would have on their feelings of neglect and abandonment—but back to Maronites and Copts.

Understanding the deep sensitivities Maronites and other Christians from Lebanon might have to being combined unreservedly with neighboring communities in the region who share their faith, but not their history, marks the beginning of fathoming a crucial reality pertaining to Middle Eastern Christianity: that there are in fact two distinct historical experiences—two separate narratives—defining the development of these indigenous Christian communities of the Arab and Islamic East. What differentiates these two broad narratives from one another is the degree of genuine personal and collective freedom experienced over time in each. The human end products of these two very different courses of historical development for native Christians are two markedly unique types in terms of their outlooks, expectations, aspirations, and self-understanding. For those Christians who have tasted freedom and struggled hard throughout the centuries to attain and preserve it, being classified unceremoniously with others of their kind who unfortunately lack any meaningful appreciation for such free existence becomes tantamount to an insult. Thus these two disparate experiences of Christians in the Middle East can be termed respectively *dhimmi* and free.

The overwhelming majority of Christian Arabs—over 90 percent—live today in *dhimmi* communities. These include the Christians in Egypt (Copts); Iraq (Chaldeans and Assyrians); Syria, Jordan, and the Palestinian territories (mainly Greek Orthodox and Melkites); and other scattered parts of the Gulf and North Africa. Extending the scope a little further in both place and time they would also comprise Christians in Iran and Turkey as well as the now vanished Christian communities in Arabia. The word *"dhimmi"* literally means in Arabic someone who lives "under the protection of" (*fi dhimmat*) Muslims. In fact it is more like subjugation under Muslim legal and political rule and entails a consequent reduction to second-class status. The term "dhimmitude" has been coined in English to indicate this form of subjugation.[6]

During the early period of Islamic conquests these Christian communities were dominated and subjugated thereby being forced to give up an existence in liberty and to succumb to dhimmitude in their own ancestral lands. Both Christians and Jews are referred to in the Koran as "People of the Book" rendering them superior in the eyes of Muslims to outright pagans because they did receive some sort of divine revelation even though they later garbled their sacred texts and went astray. For this reason they are not considered as equal to Muslims and they are granted the chance to convert or to leave the territories of the expanding House of Islam. Those who choose to stay and adhere to their religious faith are therefore reduced to *dhimmi* status and only tolerated as such. Although the Koran exhibits a pervasive fixation on Christianity when, for example, it stresses the absolute unity of God (Allah), admonishes notions of God having been begotten or himself begetting, and rejects as a particularly odious form of idolatry any hint of *shirk* (introducing external associates into the One Godhead—a clear reference to the Christian Trinity), Koranic verses vary in their severity toward Christians. Side by side with verses that call for battling the unbelievers and that consign these to the fires of eternal damnation are verses of a milder and more accepting tone: "no compulsion is there in religion" and, in a characteristic expression of Islamic fatalistic resignation, "if thy Lord had willed, whoever is in the earth would have believed."[7]

From the dawn of the Islamic period means had to be devised in the form of specific rules to accommodate the presence of these *dhimmi* minority communities within the House of Islam. The Caliph Omar is credited with first organizing and promulgating these rules, known henceforth as the Pact of Omar, which would govern the daily life of *dhimmis* and their relations with Muslims. Together these rules acted as suffocating restrictions on *dhimmis* underscoring their social and legal inferiority with respect to their Muslim masters. This religious apartheid was the price *dhimmis* had to pay to earn "protection," or the right not to be killed.

To be a *dhimmi* meant first for a Christian paying a special poll tax (the *jizya*, literally "penalty tax") for being permitted to remain an infidel under Islamic rule. He could not build new churches nor renovate dilapidated old ones. Christian houses had to be constructed lower than those of Muslims with low entrances to force the occupants to stoop when passing through them. Such measures had the purpose of keeping *dhimmis* in a continuous state of humiliation before Muslims. In addition, *dhimmi* Christians had to shave the front of their heads, don certain colored clothing, ride sideways on their donkeys or mules, salute Muslims when passing, and generally stick to the side streets and alleys where they held their funeral and other religious processions in silence. Strictly forbidden as public manifestations of *kufr* (infidelity) were the ringing of church bells, the display of crosses and other religious symbols, or loud singing during church services. Moreover, *dhimmi* Christians were not allowed to sell alcohol or carry any weapons and they were exempt from military service. They enjoyed no political rights whatsoever and usually held menial jobs or served in low-level bureaucratic posts that often required technical or linguistic expertise. Their testimony was not accepted in court in cases involving a Muslim. They were permitted their own courts for settling matters of personal status such as disputes, divorce, and inheritance. Lastly, a *dhimmi* man could not marry a Muslim woman, but a Muslim man could marry a *dhimmi* woman, who of course had to convert to Islam and raise her children in that faith.[8]

For centuries *dhimmis* throughout the lands of the Middle East lived under these debilitating restrictions. They lost all sense of what it meant to experience a life of true liberty. These communities were compelled by the Muslim majority to taste in perpetuity the bitter fruits of the initial defeat they had suffered when

Islam first prevailed in their territories through the sword. With the entry in the late eighteenth and early nineteenth centuries into the Islamic Ottoman world of such Enlightenment concepts as equality and citizenship and individual rights, a seeming paradox occurred: the more these liberal European ideas found expression in reforms and imperial decrees issued by various sultans throughout the nineteenth century, the greater was the vicious backlash on both the popular and official levels that took the form of massacres perpetrated against Christian minority communities. Examples include the Christians of Damascus in 1860; the Armenians in 1895, 1909, and 1915; the Syriac-speaking Christians of southern Anatolia in 1915 and 1918; and the Assyrians and Chaldeans in southeastern Turkey and northern Iraq in 1915 and again in 1933. In fact there was no paradox here: Muslims, whether the mob or the ruling elite, were outraged at the deliberate violation of their centuries-old system of dhimmitude through the sudden introduction of the idea of equality between them and their non-Muslim subordinates. The same thing happened later in the twentieth century when many *dhimmi* strictures were abolished from practice in certain Arab countries and *sharia*-based legal systems were diluted by being infused with European codes. Scapegoating the native Christians out of frustration at Western ideas or policies or incursions of various sorts became a recurring practice, and the attacks in recent years on Egypt's Copts or Iraq's Chaldeans and Assyrians are best understood in this gloomy context.

Much has been written by Western historians of a generation ago and earlier, only to be echoed more recently by assorted academic and journalistic apologists, about the purported tolerance of the *dhimmi* system. From the start it has been a specious argument, and such romanticized portraits of dhimmitude are thankfully on the way to being thoroughly demythologized.[9] The *dhimmi* system may have produced "protection" in the short run, precariously and at an exorbitant price, but over time it acted as a recipe for dehumanization, inferiorization, marginalization, and gradual liquidation of the targeted communities. The ultimate objective of this stifling system is *hidaya* (bringing the lost to the right path). Many *dhimmis* eventually came to prefer conversion to Islam and renunciation of their faith in order to escape the imposed hardships of dhimmitude. Those who stuck it out as *dhimmis* incurred subtle psychological damage that distorted their view of themselves and their oppressors. They began to detest calls for greater liberty coming from free Christians in the region for fear of rocking the boat. Using what is akin to casuistic circumlocution, some started to rationalize native brands of authoritarianism and lay all the blame for their woes squarely on the West. A few even reached the point of embracing their tormentors in a desperate act that can only be described as a form of collective Stockholm Syndrome. This *dhimmi* personality with its peculiar mindset is easily detectible by the freer Christians of the region and is generally despised and shunned. The scars of psychological conditioning resulting from prolonged dhimmitude have endured in the victim communities long after any political and/or legal liberalization had taken place in certain Islamic countries.

The free Christians native to the Middle East—some 8–10 percent of the total number of Christians in the region—are to be found almost exclusively in Lebanon and Cyprus. The Cypriot saga, fascinating and significant in its own right because it exhibits many of the same elements plaguing the turbulent relations between Arab Christians and their wider Islamic milieu, requires a separate investigation to do it justice. This leaves Lebanon where the Christians there, spearheaded by the Maronites, constituted until recent decades more than half the population of the country—today, they number around a third. Theirs is the other, the second and free narrative besides that of the bulk of Middle Eastern Christians, the *dhimmis*.

Lebanon is a small but mountainous country in the Eastern Mediterranean whose rugged topography offered a natural barrier to devastating external invasions and tight imperial control, especially during the pre-technological era. It consequently became attractive as a sanctuary for many beleaguered and persecuted regional ethno-religious minority groups. One of these, the Maronites, followers of an early fourth-century Christian mystic named Maron, moved into the Lebanese mountains from points north in present-day Syria and southern Turkey.[10] By 1180 they had renounced their Monothelite belief (that Christ has one divine will) and entered into full communion with the Roman Catholic Church. This gave them advantages over other regional Christian sects, not least in terms of openness to Europe and better educational opportunities for their monks and clergy. Throughout the centuries the Maronites, along with scattered members of other Christian communities adjacent to them who chose to cast their lot with them, resisted with checkered success the specter of dhimmitude and managed, at great cost in terms of blood and resources, to preserve a modicum of free and vibrant Christian existence in a Muslim ocean dotted with islands of *dhimmis*.

One indicator of the stark difference setting apart *dhimmi* and free Christian existence in the Middle East surfaces when comparison is made between Lebanon's Christians and, say, the Christians of Syria and Iraq under the nominally secular and repressive minority Baathist regimes of the late Hafez Assad and Saddam Hussein. For purposes of survival these regimes assumed an opportunistic attitude with respect to Islam and often found it useful to ease slightly the tight grip on Christians in their realm by relying on them in sensitive political and military posts. This limited and ephemeral freedom these otherwise *dhimmi* Christians were granted now and then based on the arbitrary expedience of the dictator, and never backed by legal frameworks or democratic institutions, became highly prized by them and viewed as a qualitative leap forward. By contrast, any diminution no matter how slight of the hard-won free existence of Lebanon's Christians, as happened brutally during the 1975–90 Lebanon war and was enshrined in the Saudi-sponsored and U.S.-backed Taif agreement to terminate hostilities, has been regarded by the embattled community as nothing less than a historical catastrophe. Freedom's scarcity breeds a euphoric appreciation for its sudden appearance in the minutest of quantities; while freedom's relative abundance when subjected to even modest setbacks produces existential panic and a profound sense of loss.

Another example illustrating the utterly opposed perspectives of free Christians and *dhimmis* occurred in 1996 when the leader of the Coptic Orthodox Church in Egypt, Pope Shenouda, accompanied by an entourage of representatives of other Middle Eastern churches, paid a visit to Lebanon in the spirit of ecumenical openness and inter-Christian dialogue. The visit might have proceeded flawlessly and perhaps heralded the start of a new age of understanding among the region's diverse Christian denominations had it not been marred by an unfortunate, and deliberate, oversight. Shenouda and the other visitors insisted on driving to the southern Lebanese town of Qana where earlier that year over a hundred Muslim civilians who had taken refuge inside a U.N. tent had died as a result of Israeli shelling. On the way to Qana the visitors had to pass along the coastal highway next to the Christian towns of Damour, Jiyya, Naameh, and others in the Sidon area where horrible atrocities had taken place during the Lebanon war against the inhabitants resulting in thousands of Christian deaths and an untold number of people forced to flee their destroyed houses and burning villages. Not a single word of condemnation was uttered by the illustrious visitors, who made it a point when in south Lebanon, and later in Beirut, to attack Israeli inhumanity, highlight the tragedy at Qana, and engage in the habitual political declarations against the Jewish state. This type of discourse is deemed by *dhimmis* to be far safer than throwing the spotlight on wholesale massacres of Christians and destruction of their churches and villages perpetrated by armed Palestinians supported by local Muslims. Free Christians in Lebanon felt particularly offended by this aspect of Shenouda's trip and were not amused at the gratuitous display of dhimmitude.

Freedom makes all the difference, and the jealously guarded freedoms painstakingly secured by Lebanon's Christians have set them apart in a positive sense from the rest of their Arab surroundings, including their *dhimmi* brethren. A community's free and secure existence must act as a necessary prerequisite for any creative role or constructive mission expected of that community vis-à-vis its wider environment. As long as Christians in Lebanon remained relatively free and secure they were able to lead in the Arab cultural and intellectual renaissance at the turn of the twentieth century; they could through daily peaceful interaction over decades with their Muslim Lebanese neighbors osmotically mold many of them into exceptionally liberal-minded and modern individuals who have stood out among other Muslims in the Arab region; and they managed to serve as local and regional agents for progress through a determined and sustained emphasis on education and publishing, advanced medical care, innovative commercial and banking prowess, and a vibrant entertainment industry.

Beirut, despite the devastating battering it endured for over three decades since 1975, remains today the Arab world's freest and on many levels its most exciting city. The correlation between free Christianity in Lebanon and the open and cosmopolitan appeal of the country's capital is undeniable. But more pertinently, Beirut continues to be the breathing lungs for Arab and other Christians as far afield as Turkey, Armenia, and Iran. The greater Beirut area contains a plethora of denominational apostolates and bishoprics that are in direct daily contact with their native communities throughout the entire Middle East and beyond. These ecclesiastical headquarters serve as listening posts for the conditions, grievances, and aspirations of all indigenous Middle Eastern Christians who look to Beirut as both their outlet to freedom and their barometer for impending danger. In short, the better off Lebanon's free Christians are, the more easily the rest of the region's Christians can breathe.[11]

In a tough environment like the Middle East all politics on a deeper level is really a matter of survival, and survival often translates into adapting to unpleasant realities as a first step to resisting, if not changing, them. With a rare commodity like freedom in this freedom-starved part of the world comes a responsibility of momentous and historic proportions. Regrettably, the political as well as spiritual leaders of Lebanon's free Christians have not always lived up to the required level of responsibility that the preservation of the precious freedoms of their community demands. They have wallowed in petty personal and parochial disputes over issues of prominence and power when they should have been unified in focusing on the perils surrounding them from all sides. They have indulged in venal excesses and all kinds of corruption when they were called upon to inspire their followers with the loftiest of ethical principles and behavior. Thus they have consistently failed to live up to the fateful historical task with which they were entrusted, namely the defense of the free existence of their toiling community. And yet, in the face of all odds, an emasculated and weary freedom has survived in Lebanon—but for how long?

III. REASONS FOR DEMOGRAPHIC DECLINE

Unlike the other two faiths, Islam and Judaism, Christianity does not attach salvific significance to holy places. Yes, Rome is important for Catholics as are shrines of saints, and the Holy Land where the Incarnate God walked and lived and taught and suffered and rose on the third day carries tremendous spiritual significance for all Christian believers. However, reclaiming and maintaining political control over such areas, or undertaking a pilgrimage to these revered places as an unavoidable requirement for being a Christian in good standing—the erroneous obsessions perhaps of a bygone era when building Christendom as a theocracy was the overriding priority—do not constitute the essence of faith in Christ, who is infinitely more important than any place, and who remains perpetually accessible without the mediation of venues.

Consider, for example, the frustrated outburst of a Serbian taxi driver who told a BBC correspondent in the summer of 2009: "Kosovo is ours. It has always been and always will be. And if the West doesn't like it, to hell with them."[12] This is not to be taken as a dogmatic theological expression of Serbian Orthodox doctrine—it emanates, rather, from a curious mix of nationalism, historical tradition, emotions, and popular spirituality tinged with defiance against the backdrop of the traumatic events of recent years in the Balkans. This is not to belittle national churches around the world—for example, the intense attachment of Catholic Irish to Ireland, or the Polish Catholic Church to Poland, or Lebanon's Maronites to Mount Lebanon, or the Russian Orthodox faithful to Mother Russia—but in none of these instances does such an organic connection to locale per se constitute a necessary pillar of the faith in question.[13]

Dispossession involving expulsion or forced exile from one's homeland is a very harsh punishment indeed for anyone regardless of creed. But voluntary departure through emigration, under pressure (the push factor), or in response to better prospects elsewhere (the pull factor), coupled with endemic elements that retard demographic growth, are features peculiar to the Middle Eastern Christian predicament. Demographic attrition for these Christians has come through a variety of channels. Generally speaking, and except in the remote backward villages where life is still largely agrarian, birthrates among Middle Eastern Christians tend to be lower than those of their Muslim counterparts. One reason might be a pervasive communal desire to provide their children with a good education, which is costly under the best of circumstances, thereby imposing limits on the number of offspring per household. Another reason may have to do with a more widespread use of birth-control measures among Christians despite admonitions of such practices coming from Catholic ecclesiastical authorities. A related socioeconomic reason is that many of the urban Christians are, or aspire to be, middle-class professionals or owners of small businesses, especially in the Levant, and this too favors compact nuclear families. Add to these elements the sociological fact that Christians only accept monogamy as the basis of marriage, unlike the prevalence of polygamy in certain Islamic settings throughout the region like parts of Egypt, Saudi Arabia, and the Gulf. Moreover, divorce in most regional Christian denominations is not an easy option but instead is generally discouraged or encumbered with deliberate obstacles. Scientifically reliable statistics supporting these assertions are hard to come by on a region-wide scale and are utterly absent for certain specific sub-areas; however, the reasons and factors outlined here do reflect an accurate picture of the level of overall demographic trends and communal conditions.

There are additional structural reasons pertaining to the internal makeup of these Christian communities of the Middle East that have contributed to retarding their demographic growth. These include a dearth of historic statesman–like leadership possessing a bold vision for their community and able to converse with, and impress, the powers that be in the outside world on the highest levels; deep and lingering sectarian differences and divisions crippling collective awakening and concerted action; the relative isolation and parochialism of some (the Copts) and the feudal-clannish and mercantile disposition of others (the Levantine Christians). These and other similar features over time are not conducive to normal healthy population increases, mainly because they shake all confidence in the future and instill the feeling that life is tenuous by cultivating a pervading sense of uncertainty and foreboding about impending calamities.

The *dhimmi*/free divide has meant, among other things, poor or nonexistent communication, coordination, or understanding between these two dissimilar traditions of Christian life in the East. Hardly any common ground exists that would generate a set of shared priorities regarding the threats facing them, or a unified plan of action for the future on matters of destiny for these communities. Even among the *dhimmi* communities themselves, who constitute the vast majority of the region's Christians, there is precious little appreciation for one another's plights, or any concrete attempts to face similar dangers concertedly. For instance, on the whole, Iraqi Christians did not react to the recurrent attacks on the Copts in recent years, nor did these Copts voice any significant protests concerning the violence that has befallen the Christians of Iraq since 2003. This lack of any regional solidarity and unity of purpose among Christians—where *dhimmis* and their freer coreligionists eye each other with mutual unsettled incomprehension, and where *dhimmis* have become so domesticated they will resist attracting attention to themselves under any circumstances—has left these communities vulnerable to the inevitable, and haphazard, blows of decay and disintegration.

The principal cause of Christian demographic decline in the Arab and surrounding Middle East—the great reducer—is emigration, and it doesn't take much to trigger it. The economic disruption brought on by years of war caused many Lebanese, the majority of these being Christians, to leave their war-torn country after 1975, first to neighboring Cyprus, then to Europe, the Americas, and Australia in search of security and better livelihood. The Lebanese Christians, in particular the youth, have a tradition of emigrating in large numbers when economic prospects falter or when their community is directly targeted with violence. During the First World War the Ottoman

Turks perpetrated widespread atrocities in Lebanon and caused a devastating famine. It is estimated anecdotally that one-third of the population perished, one-third emigrated, and one-third remained. Whether or not these are accurate percentages, what is beyond doubt is that a huge wave of emigration took place from Lebanon at that time, and it overwhelmingly involved Christians.

During the 1990s and early twenty-first century the Persian Gulf became a great economic magnet for the region's educated and newly graduated youth including many Christians. It proved convenient because it was close to their home countries of mainly Lebanon, Jordan, Iraq, and the Palestinian territories, and no one had the intention of quitting home permanently to emigrate to, and settle in, the Gulf. These would be stints measured in a few short years of intense work and, it was hoped, wealth accumulation to be followed by a return home to get established and raise a family. With the sudden onset of the global economic and financial crisis and its tsunami-like impact on Dubai and other parts of the Gulf, many of these talented Christian Arab youth found themselves jobless virtually overnight with few prospects awaiting them back in their countries of origin. Consequently, large numbers have ended up leaving for the West where they will most likely remain for good. Since reliance on regular remittances from family members working abroad is a time-honored practice among quite a few Middle Eastern Christian communities, the need to constantly seek opportunities away from home to satisfy this expectation fuels emigration. Add to this the seductive brain-drain aspect of the West that magnetically attracts and absorbs young talent from all over the world, and the relative ease of assimilation for incoming Christians in a milieu where the same worldview they espouse is thriving within advanced secular democratic societies, and one begins to grasp the powerful effects of emigration on the depletion of indigenous Christians from the troubled and unstable Middle East.

Emigration has a phenomenology unto itself based on the twin elements of amorphous allure and the illusion of assured success waiting to be achieved just beyond the horizon. Naturally, not everyone who emigrates succeeds overseas despite at times strenuous efforts, and many of those who fail do not find repatriation to their country of origin automatic or easy. The results are hardships, unpredictable transformations, identity crises, regrets, rootlessness, and irreversible deracination. Eventual assimilation, if it occurs, is never arrived at smoothly, at least not for the first generation of emigrants. Even for those who "do well" and "make it" in their adopted land there lingers the subterranean angst born of having cut themselves off from authentic roots and the security of existential anchorage.

But what is one to do when imminent danger of death and destruction wells up from every direction and all avenues of hope for a peaceful future appear blocked? It is principally the violence visited sporadically upon these Christian communities in their native towns and villages across the Middle East, and the absence of any reliable means of protection in a region seething with religious fanaticism and despotic forms of rule, which impels Christians to flee and not return. The crux of the problem for these native Christians lies in the resurgence of precisely this Islamic religious fanaticism, or Islamism. This phenomenon has been given a variety of names: fundamentalism, militant extremism, Islamism, Jihadism, Political Islam, radical Islam, Salafism, and more—but essentially they all boil down to the same thing for non-Muslims: intolerance, hostility, and violence.

Today's Middle East is a different place than it was two generations ago. Take a look, for instance, at any black-and-white photograph of the legendary Egyptian singer Um Kulthoom in concert in Egypt from the middle decades of the last century, or any similar public performance from that era, and you will at once notice that none of the women in the audience wore veils or distinctive Islamic headdress. Pictures of such performances today will invariably show a large number of the females attending with their heads, if not more, totally covered. Egypt was a more liberal society in the early twentieth century than at the outset of the twenty-first. This regression is due mostly to societal pressures emanating from Islamist movements entrenched in the country with deep roots and an extended reach. Hasan al-Banna (1906–1949), founder of the Muslim Brotherhood in Egypt, and Sayyid Qutb (1906–1966), the ideologue and theoretician of the broader fundamentalist-Islamist revival, have constituted jointly the cornerstone first of the Egyptian variety of Islamism, and later of much of the Jihadist ideology permeating the Muslim world, which has inspired suicide bombings, mass-casualty terrorism, and televised beheadings. Both these men openly rejected the secular infusions of socialist, nationalist, and liberal ideas coming into Arab intellectual circles from the West in favor of a return to a purist interpretation of Islam based on the strict application of *sharia* (Islamic law) and an emphasis on the antagonistic dualism of *Dar al-Islam* (the House of Islam where Muslims are the majority and exercise political control) and *Dar al-Harb* (the House of War where *kufr*, or infidelity, reigns and needs to be constantly battled). Western ideological influences were thus viewed by them as mental expressions of that detested colonialism and imperialism of the infidels, enemies of Allah and his Prophet. Only a rebirth of true Islam touching every facet of life will offer the best resistance to this imported, or externally imposed, corruption. Banna's Muslim Brotherhood launched a pervasive internal reform of Islam along fundamentalist lines and did not hesitate to advocate violence as a necessary means of change, while Qutb's brief sojourn in the America of the 1940s was enough to convince him that there could be no reconciliation with the House of War, and that all unbelievers, including Christians and Jews, had to be subdued as a prelude to being converted or killed.[14]

Contributing to the success in recent decades of Islamist movements to attract followers among Muslim youth and become established across Muslim societies as a force not to be trifled with have been the perceived failures of secular ideologies like Arab nationalism, pan-Arabism, and Nasserism. The bitter fruits of these ideologies, as seen through an Islamist prism, have been the authoritarian regimes of Arab states that repress their peoples and act as Western surrogates inside the House of Islam. Add to this the worsening socioeconomic conditions in many Arab states in which populations have been on the increase while the rift separating rich and poor has continued to widen, and nothing of innovative significance is being invented and produced by Arabs that the rest of the world is queuing up to acquire. Lastly, one must throw in what is seen by the extremists as American acquiescence in continued Palestinian suffering. The stage has thus been set for the Islamists to seize the initiative and challenge the status quo everywhere in the Muslim world with a penchant to use violence to further their ends.

Historically, Islamists rely on a long tradition of conservative jurisprudential exegesis purporting to go all the way back to the *sahaba* (the Prophet's companions), and the "righteous *salaf*," meaning the uncontaminated early beginnings of the new faith. Of the four schools of Sunni Muslim Koranic interpretation, the Hanbali following the jurist Ahmed Ibn Hanbal

(780–855), represents the most rigid and least tolerant, and it is to this tradition, through later scholarly luminaries like Ibn Taymiyya (1263–1328) and his disciple Ibn Qayyim al-Jawziyya (1292–1350), that present-day Islamists turn for guidance in formulating their radical *fatwas* (authoritative religious rulings) regarding infidels and non-believers, Christians included. This same tradition, with its unbending derogatory views of Christians as well as those Muslims displaying a milder disposition, was rekindled and rendered more extreme with the emergence in Arabia of Sheikh Mohammad Ibn Abdel-Wahhab (1703–1792), whose alliance with the desert tribal chief Mohammad Ibn Saud (d. 1765) was the basis for the eventual formation of the Kingdom of Saudi Arabia. Wahhabism, as this intensified expression of the Hanbali tradition came to be designated, is the ideological milk on which Osama Bin Laden was reared. Not only does it entail a strict adherence to *sharia* including punishment by death for apostasy and the severing of limbs for other offenses, but it also bristles with aversion toward the slightest odor of *shirk* and other traces of idolatry. In Abdel-Wahhab's time, calls for *tawheed* (emphasis on the absolute unity of God) and relentless stripping of all ornaments from the *Kaaba* (the black stone of Mecca toward which Muslims pray) were accompanied by periodic raids into predominantly Shiite southern Iraq to destroy tombs and relics of holy men and to desecrate similar sites deemed sacred. *Takfir* (declaring a person or group, including coreligionists, to be infidels) was the Wahhabi way with respect to Shiites, moderate Muslims, and all non-Muslims, and it was usually followed by violent attacks in the spirit of Jihad.[15]

On the Sunni side of the Islamic sectarian spectrum today the Taliban, Al Qaeda, and other offshoot Salafi-Takfiri Jihadists constitute the greatest threat to the Christian communities native to parts of the Arab and Islamic world. But Wahhabism and its modern Salafist derivatives are matched at times by Shiite extremism, especially since the success of Ayatollah Khomeini's Islamic revolution in Iran in 1979. A militant apocalyptic version of Twelver Shiism emerging from Qom in Iran and spreading to parts of the Shiite communities of Islam—constituting about 15 percent of all Muslims worldwide—follows the religious directives of the Supreme Jurist-Consult (*Wilayat al-Faqih*), who is the spiritual leader of the Iranian revolution and Khomeini's successor.

Comparing these two versions of Islamist militancy from the vantage point of their respective damaging impacts on the region's Christians is instructive because it discloses something of an asymmetry in favor of the Shiites. While both the Sunni Salafists and the Shiite followers of *Wilayat al-Faqih* have as their ultimate aim the establishment of a fundamentalist Islamic state where dhimmitude, if it is in fact granted to them, would be the best option Christians could hope for, these Christians are likely to fare better under Shiite rule than in a country run by Sunni Salafis. The proof of this proposition is simple and straightforward: Christian churches and their trace communities still exist in today's Mullah-dominated Iran, but any native Christianity has long ago been eradicated from the territory that constitutes the Wahhabi Kingdom of Saudi Arabia.

Again, comparing the Sunni Islamist Palestinian paramilitary movement Hamas, currently entrenched in the Gaza Strip, with its Shiite Iran–inspired counterpart in Lebanon, Hezbollah, one can see that the former still actively seeks, through its ongoing struggle with Israel, to create a future Islamist Palestine, while the latter, Hezbollah, has long ago discovered the futility of such a project in the sectarian-riddled Lebanese context and has consequently plunged into the labyrinthine world of internal Lebanese confessional politics by forming political alliances with Christians, Druze, and others, and by confining its resistance focus to the small stretch of Israeli-occupied Lebanese territory, the Shebaa Farms, in the south. What brings together these two strange bedfellows, Hezbollah and some of Lebanon's Christians, is a shared fear they have of the prospect of some 400,000 mostly Sunni Palestinian refugees becoming naturalized Lebanese citizens. Should it happen, such a development would be detrimental for Lebanon's delicate and already strained demographic balance among its various sectarian communal components. We have here essentially two minorities in the wider Sunni-majority Islamic world—Shiites and Christians—joining hands to confront a renewed bid for Sunni hegemony. It needs to be added here that historically, Lebanon's Christians have witnessed very few instances of Shiite violence directed against them, whereas over the decades and centuries such violence was brought down upon their communities re-currently by Druze and Sunnis.

A competition of sorts seems underway across the Middle East between Sunni and Shiite radicalism in which Saudi Arabia and Iran are vying with one another Cold War–style for re-gional influence, and countries like Egypt and Syria are taking opposite sides in this unfolding regional polarization along broad Islamic sectar-ian lines. The net effect of this radicalization is highly undermining to native Christian wellbe-ing, not to speak of the overall intimidation fac-tor it generates that cows Muslim moderates into silence. Yet once more it is the Saudis who emerge as the more abrasive of the two con-tending sides. Direct links do exist between the regime in Tehran and an organization like Hez-bollah, but these connections have hardly ever translated into actual assaults on Christians, whether in Lebanon or elsewhere in the region. Such direct links may be non-existent, or difficult to establish, between the Saudi authorities and various Salafi or Takfiri extremists who do actively target Christian and other groups; however, the vast reserves of petrodollars the Saudis have expended over the years to promote and disseminate their virulent and potentially violent version of Wahhabi Islam through a growing global network of *madrassas* (Koranic schools) that only teach the Koran as interpreted by Jihadists, have resulted in the proselytizing of extremist hate globally, thereby spawning organized terrorism. The "special" or "strategic" relationship, as it is often described, between the United States and Saudi Arabia has for decades prior to 9/11 helped to mask this ugly reality about the Kingdom's role in nurturing the kind of hatred that exploded on that fateful day into indiscriminate mass murder of innocents on American soil. The menace of a nuclear Iran is surely very real and alarming, but the programmed seepage of poisonous Wahhabi fanaticism throughout the Muslim world remains a greater long-term threat to that world and to the rest of humanity.

The Middle East environment is rendered more lethal for Christians when alongside the Islamist extremists are factored in the authoritarian regimes that maintain a stranglehold on so many of the region's societies. Christian communities often find themselves caught in the crossfire between these two sparring rivals— the religious militants and the brutal despots. The scattering of Christians in concentrations far beyond their ancestral homes—Copts in Los Angeles, Iraqi Assyrians in Chicago, Lebanese Maronites and Palestinian Christians everywhere—is due in no small part to this deadly contest in which they invariably end up as collateral damage. Egypt's Copts are a classic case in point when it comes to being hit repeatedly from both sides of the Islamist-regime divide. In October 2005 attacks on several Coptic and other churches in Alexandria were the direct result of incitement by extremists on the Internet and inflammatory sermons at Friday prayers. When seething mobs approached to burn and pillage, the state's security forces simply stood by and did not interfere. This pattern of fanatical rabble-rousing and assault accompanied by apathy from the authorities has occurred in

47

Egypt before and since October 2005. And native non-Muslim minority communities elsewhere in the Middle East have not been immune to similar attacks and/or official indifference; just ask any Christian from Iraq or Lebanon.

Regimes also callously marginalize and mistreat their Christian communities in keeping with the *dhimmi* stigma. In Cairo the garbage cleaners are predominantly Christian (the *zabaleen*) and they used to collect the city's refuse and feed the organic matter to the pigs that they raised. During the summer of 2009, in an impulsive overreaction to the scare over the H1N1 swine flu virus, the Egyptian government ill-advisedly ordered the culling of all pigs thereby destroying the livelihood of these Christian *zabaleen*. By September Cairo was literally buried in heaps of trash.[16] Even the lowliest of Christian *dhimmis,* and their pigs, could still serve some use.

Repressive regional authoritarian regimes are mainly responsible for sustaining the Arab world's freedom deficit,[17] and for discriminating against, and sometimes persecuting, their minorities through communal scapegoating—Kurds, Shiites, Jews, Baha'is, and Christians have suffered from such abuses. But none of this was supposed to have happened had the original notions and expectations of the theoreticians who first formulated the ideologies that imparted life to these regimes been accurate or realistic. Secularism did finally make its way to Middle Eastern shores in the middle of the last century, but this was not the liberal, democratic, free-market, and humanist secularism of the West, firmly grounded in a rich tradition of personal and collective rights dating back to the eighteenth century. Instead, it was a curious blend of the violent and intolerant secularism of the socialists and ideological left mixed with its mirror image from the fascists and extreme nationalists of the far right, and transposed to a Third World setting to be manifested brutally through bloodshed and totalitarian-like rule. The men who came up with this concoction were all Greek Orthodox Christian Arabs, and their declared motivation had been to provide the Arab rulers and their masses with the potent ammunition to fight Western colonialism. Of course the deeper underlying reasons behind their ideological importations had to do with their ingrained dhimmitude.

In 1938 a book appeared entitled *The Arab Awakening* written by a Lebanese-Egyptian historian and diplomat, George Antonius (1891–1942), who was of Greek Orthodox background. It represented the first coherent depiction of the secular idea of Arab nationalism whose origins, explained the author, were rooted in the disillusionment with Western machinations in Arab lands during World War I, and whose breeding ground was the American University of Beirut and the educational input introduced through successive Protestant missions throughout the nineteenth century. A few years later another Greek Orthodox from Syria, Michel Aflaq (1910–1989), having spent time in Paris during the 1930s, crafted a synthesis between Antonius's Arab nationalism and borrowings from European socialism with the stated objective of reinforcing Arab unity in the face of Western imperial domination. The offspring was the secular ideology of Baathism, a derivative of Arab nationalism that seized control of

Iraq and Syria through cruel coups d'etat ultimately giving us Saddam Hussein and Hafez Assad.[18] It was this Arab national-socialist vision of the Antonius and Aflaq variety that a charismatic leader like Gamal Abdel Nasser could employ in the 1950s and 1960s as a means to inflame the Arab masses against the West, thereby inaugurating the era of Arab military dictatorships. As the historian and critic David Pryce-Jones has put it: "Nationalism, as rhapsodized by Aflaq and his like and manipulated with supreme skill by Nasser and others, served to legitimize aspiring one-man rulers in their bid for power."[19]

The portrait of nationalist and socialist appropriations into the Middle East would not be complete without mention of two other figures, both also Orthodox Christians: Antun Saadeh (1904–1949) and Constantine Zurayk (1909–2000). Saadeh, a Lebanese who spent part of his early childhood in South America, founded the Syrian National Social Party under influences from fascist and other extreme European nationalist groups. His party emphasized a distinctive Syrian cultural-racial type and on that basis called for unity of the Fertile Crescent. Saadeh himself was eventually accused of treason by the Lebanese authorities, hastily tried, and executed; however, his party has persisted as a secondary player on the Lebanese political scene. Zurayk, a Syrian diplomat and academician who taught for years at the American University of Beirut, is considered the latter-day philosopher of Arab nationalism who made the Palestinian cause after 1967 the centerpiece of Arab politics and Arab resistance to Israeli and Western hegemony.[20]

These four men and others of their ilk were embodiments of an intellectual dhimmitude whose primary obsession was to discover, or fabricate if need be, a secular unifier of Christians and Muslims that transcended religious differences and antagonisms, and that would shield the vulnerable minorities from the wrath of the majority. Their varying, often grandiose, permutations of the Arab nationalist, or Arabist, project resemble the aspiration once harbored by many Jews desiring to overcome the Jew-Gentile distinction when they gravitated in droves toward Marxism, which offered them the chance to eliminate religious and racial divides by joining with other revolutionaries to fight the heinous bourgeoisie. In similar fashion it was hoped the common secular platform of Arabism would erase sectarian and religious differences thereby lifting the Arab nation to a whole new level where the joint struggle would then be with other external enemies, real or contrived. It worked for a while under the secular dictatorships that hoisted the banner of Arabism—that is the fleeting period that the *dhimmi* Christians of Iraq suffering today mistakenly hark back to with pathetic nostalgia.

The fatal flaw of these Arabists, born of their obsequious *dhimmi* attitude toward Islamic requirements and priorities, lay in their misplaced choice of a secularism that necessarily had to pass through their adapted nationalist and socialist hybrids. They couldn't have borrowed more abysmally from the West. And when their ideological brew helped catapult tyrants to power, shedding pools of their own people's blood in the process, it came as no surprise—except maybe to them—to see an Islamist revival as the logical backlash. Herein lay the colossal failure in the twentieth century of the Arab intellectual class, led as it was by the likes of these *dhimmi* Christians. Now that the Islamist genie is out of the bottle, there is no going back to *dhimmi*-inspired secular ideologies only to have them once again serve as springboards for renewed regime repression. Indeed the fruits of dhimmitude are inescapably tragic.

IV. WHERE TO GO FROM HERE

Alongside Islamist fanaticism and the nasty regimes that have shown the ugly face of secularism, the Middle East's Christians have had to contend with Western indifference to their plight as targeted Christians coupled with American "pragmatism" and "realism." Fundamentally, United States policies in the Middle East have never placed a significant priority on the conditions of indigenous Christians or the threats they have been up against just for being Christian: neither in Lebanon in 1958 during the first serious instance of Christian-Muslim strife, nor again in Lebanon in 1975 or after, nor in southern Sudan during twenty years of civil war, nor in Iraq since 2003, nor at any time with respect to Egypt's Copts. There is an ingrained culture in Washington's foreign policy establishment that prefers to avoid addressing the existential phobias of the region's Christians. These beleaguered Christian communities have become marginalized in American strategic thinking and hence expendable next to larger and more pressing economic, political, and security interests.

For their part these native Christians, whether *dhimmi* or free, have lost confidence in the West generally and in the United States in particular. They sense that Europe has shown occasional sensitivity to their dire situation, but they know well Europe's limitations in this regard: having itself become largely a post-Christian continent; laboring under severe problems of procreation and Islamic immigration; and lacking the raw power and international clout of the United States. The Vatican, particularly under Pope John-Paul II, showed sustained interest in the embattled Christians of Lebanon and the disappearing Palestinian Christians, and that Pope set up a special synod for the Maronite Church. Pope Benedict XVI, after a May 2009 visit to the Holy Land, announced in September another special synod scheduled for 2010 to deal with challenges confronting the Middle East's Catholic churches.

But popes have no military divisions, as Stalin wryly remarked; still, no Christian in the region seriously entertains the prospect of fleets arriving from the West to subdue their oppressors and save them—these are the fanciful accusations leveled at Christians by their detractors, mainly in the Western media. The primary challenge for Middle Eastern Christians is how to remain in organic communion on the deepest levels of the mind and the spirit with the West while concurrently protecting themselves from the inevitable kicks and stabs—intentional or otherwise—that will come at them from this same West, and how to do all this while not compromising their authentic belonging to the native soil of the East from where they sprang.

A tall order perhaps, but one thing is certain: constant bypassing of them and their legitimate concerns by American policymakers is not going to lead those Christians who decide to stay in their ancestral lands to commit individual or collective suicide.

A true Christian believer living under any circumstances can never be robbed of the joy, the inner peace, and the incredible freedom bestowed by that faith. On this level the categories of *dhimmi* and free, which relate essentially to life in this world, simply do not apply. A profound comprehension of the theology of the Cross knows that it leads straight to the Resurrection. But using any of this to preach cynically to Middle Eastern Christians that therefore they ought not to resist dhimmitude is a cruel double-standard that free persons elsewhere would not apply to themselves were their freedoms to be placed in jeopardy.

Despite the bleak tapestry of contracting numbers and a swelling mass of *dhimmis*, there are glimmers of good news for the Middle East's long-suffering Christians. There is tangible evidence in many Christian communities across the region of spiritual renewal among the youth. In Lebanon, for instance, where freedom of worship and freedom to proselytize remain intact unlike in the rest of the Arab world, vocations to the priesthood are rising, and this unadvertised fact is causing an over-flow of such callings to neighboring Christian communities. Such a phenomenon is bound to guarantee the persistence of Christians rooted indefinitely in their native Middle Eastern environment.

Outsiders are free to wash their hands of these Christians; however, certain steps that are not costly if undertaken could help advance the interests of both the Islamic societies and the wider world at large. Nurturing settled, stable, prosperous, and reasonably free and secure na-tive Christian communities in the Middle East has served in many instances as a factor pro-moting Islamic openness and moderation. Such moderation is sure to be strengthened when Muslims interact daily with confident fel-low-native adherents to a creed that does not condone suicide bombers, respects women, is not out for religious domination, upholds the principle of religious pluralism, is compatible with liberal democracy, defends personal and group rights, emphasizes the centrality of education, and is not uncomfortable with many features of secular modern living. Whenever local Christians have felt relatively unmolested, they have acted as catalysts for positive change and conduits for some of the West's finest and most enduring universal values, and this in turn has advanced Islamic tolerance and moderation.

What Muslims living in the West demand for themselves—and receive—by way of rights and legal protections they ought to be ready to grant to Christians living in Muslim-majority countries. Reciprocity in these vital matters creates the optimal conditions for productive civilizational dialogue. Promoting democracy among Muslims that stresses minority rights, contemplating boldly federal options for local autonomy, and supporting benign liberal secularism wherever feasible—these would be ingredients for a roadmap toward anchoring a healthy pluralism in the Middle East.

NOTES

1. 1 Corinthians 1:23.

2. Ethan Bonner, "Christianity Losing Its Force in Mideast," *International Herald Tribune*, May 13, 2009.

3. Homily by His Holiness Benedict XVI during the Mass at the Josafat Valley, Jerusalem, May 12, 2009. See http://www.vatican.va/holy_father/benedict_xvi/homilies/2009/documents/hf_ben-xvi_hom_20090512_josafat-valley_en.html.

4. Matthew 5:44.

5. For the full transcript of the President's Cairo speech see www.nytimes.com2009/06/04/US/politics/04obama.text.html.

6. For the best discussion to date on dhimmitude see Bat Ye'or, *The Decline of Eastern Christianity under Islam: From Jihad to Dhimmitude, Seventh–Twentieth Centuries,* translated from French by Miriam Kochan and David Littman (Madison, NJ: Fairleigh Dickinson University Press, 1996).

7. See Koran, sura of The Cow, 162 and 255; sura of The Table, 81 and 109ff; sura of Jonah, 98; sura of Sincere Religion, 1; and sura of The Bee, 85ff. See also Habib C. Malik, "Political Islam and the Roots of Violence," in *The Influence of Faith: Religious Groups and U.S. Foreign Policy,* edited by Elliott Abrams, The Ethics and Public Policy Center (Lanham, MD: Rowman & Littlefield Publishers, Inc., 2001).

8. On *dhimmi* restrictions see, as an example, Efraim Karsh, *Islamic Imperialism: A History* (New Haven, CT: Yale University Press, 2006), pp. 25–26.

9. Renowned Western scholars of Islam such as Sir Hamilton Gibb, William Montgomery Watt, Jacques Augustin Berque, Maxime Rodinson, Marshall Hodgson, Rev. Kenneth Cragg, and the Georgetown duo John L. Esposito and John O. Voll—to name just a few—have all either peddled the myth of dhimmitude as tolerance, or downplayed its destructive effects on its victims. Refreshing deconstructions of such appeasement views have come recently from Bat Ye'or, Daniel Pipes, Robert Spencer, George Weigel, and Ibn Warraq.

10. On the Maronites see a study in French that just appeared by Ray Jabre Mouawad entitled *Les Maronites, chretiens du Liban* (Beirut: La Librairie Antoine, 2009).

11. On Beirut's centrality for the region's Christians see Habib C. Malik, "The Future of Christian Arabs" in *Mediterranean Quarterly: A Journal of Global Issues* 2, no. 2 (spring 1991), pp. 72–84.

12. BBC broadcast, July 18, 2009.

13. For example, the near-apocalyptic dispute between Islam and Judaism over the Al Aqsa Mosque (the Temple Mount for Jews) is something alien to an authentic Christian temperament. There was a time when Christians strayed into that murky territory—the idolatry of place—and lived to regret it.

14. See Brynjar Lia, *The Society of the Muslim Brothers in Egypt* (Reading, UK: Ithaca Press, 1998); and on Qutb

see Robert Irwin, "Is This the Man Who Inspired Bin Laden?" in the *Guardian,* November 1, 2001. See also Gilles Kepel, *The Prophet and Pharaoh (Muslim Extremism in Egypt),* translated by John Rothschild (London: Al-Saqi Books, 1985).

15. On Hanbalism and Ibn Taymiyya see the stimulating discussion in Richard K. Khuri, *Freedom, Modernity, and Islam: Toward a Creative Synthesis* (Syracuse, NY: Syracuse University Press, 1998), pp. 167–174, 247, and 257. On Wahhabism see George Rentz, "Wahhabism and Saudi Arabia" in Derek Hopwood, editor, *The Arabian Peninsula: Society and Politics* (Totowa, NJ: Rowman & Littlefield, 1972), pp. 54–66.

16. *International Herald Tribune,* September 21, 2009.

17. See the United Nations Development Program's *Arab Human Development Report* of 2002.

18. On Antonius see Albert Hourani, "The Arab Awakening Forty Years After" in Albert Hourani, *Emergence of the Modern Middle East* (Berkeley: University of California Press, 1981), pp. 193–215; and Martin Kramer, "Ambition, Arabism, and George Antonius" in Martin Kramer, editor, *Arab Awakening and Islamic Revival: The Politics of Ideas in the Middle East* (New Brunswick, NJ: Transaction Press, 1996), pp. 112–123. On Aflaq see Youssef M. Choueiri, *Arab Nationalism: A History* (Oxford: Blackwell Publishers Ltd., 2000), pp. 154–165.

19. David Pryce-Jones, *The Closed Circle: An Interpretation of the Arabs* (New York: Harper Perennial, 1991), p. 15.

20. On Saadeh and his party see Daniel Pipes, *Greater Syria: The History of an Ambition* (New York: Oxford University Press, 1990), pp. 100ff. On Zurayk see the introductory material in George N. Atiyeh and Ibrahim M. Oweiss, editors, *Arab Civilization: Challenges and Responses: Studies in Honor of Constantine K. Zurayk* (Albany: State University of New York Press, 1988).

About the Author

Habib C. Malik was born in January 1954 in Washington, D.C., the son of Lebanese philosopher and diplomat Charles Malik. His early schooling took place in both the United States and Lebanon. He graduated in 1977 with a BA in history from the American University of Beirut after doing his senior year at Princeton University. He received his master's and PhD in modern European intellectual history from Harvard University in 1979 and 1985, respectively. He is currently an associate professor of history and cultural studies at the Lebanese American University (Byblos campus). He divides his interests between the history of Western thought and the issues and problems of his ancestral home, Lebanon, and the Middle East at large—in particular the plight of native

Christian communities, the future of freedom and democracy in Arab societies, and the challenges posed by Islamization. He is the author of *Between Damascus and Jerusalem: Lebanon and Middle East Peace* and *Receiving Søren Kierkegaard: The Early Impact and Transmission of His Thought,* and editor of *The Challenge of Human Rights: Charles Malik and the Universal Declaration,* along with many articles, essays, and book chapters in both Arabic and English on pluralism, Arab Christians, human rights, Political Islam, and the Arab reception of Kierkegaard. He lives in Lebanon just outside Beirut and is married to Hiba Costa; they have three children.

Herbert and Jane Dwight
Working Group on
Islamism and the
International Order

HOOVER INSTITUTION
STANFORD UNIVERSITY

The Herbert and Jane Dwight Working Group on Islamism and the International Order seeks to engage in the task of reversing Islamic radicalism through reforming and strengthening the legitimate role of the state across the entire Muslim world. Efforts will draw on the intellectual resources of an array of scholars and practitioners from within the United States and abroad, to foster the pursuit of modernity, human flourishing, and the rule of law and reason in Islamic lands—developments that are critical to the very order of the international system.

The Working Group is chaired by Hoover fellows Fouad Ajami and Charles Hill with an active participation of Director John Raisian. Current core membership includes Russell A. Berman, Abbas Milani, and Shelby Steele, with contributions from Zeyno Baran, Reul Marc Gerecht, Ziad Haider, R. John Hughes, Nibras Kazimi, Habib Malik, and Joshua Teitelbaum.

Index